HO

KAREN PRESS

HOME

CARCANET

First published in Great Britain in 2000 by
Carcanet Press Limited
4th Floor, Conavon Court
12-16 Blackfriars Street
Manchester M3 5BQ

A CIP catalogue record for this book
is available from the British Library
ISBN 1 85754 478 1

The publisher acknowledges financial assistance
from the Arts Council of England

Set in 10pt Garamond Simoncini by Bryan Williamson, Frome
Printed and bound in England by SRP Ltd, Exeter

Contents

Versions of some of the poems in this collection have been published in *Staffrider, New Coin, New Contrast, The Boston Review, Wasafiri, Kalahari Review, Slugnews* and *PN Review*.

Heart's Hunger

Heart's Hunger

I

I stored you against my eyelids
my treasure, more precious than water.

> Then they stole my home, my land,
> the possibility of my hands, my last dress.

I saw them, and when my eyes closed
I could not remember you.

> Hunger has eaten my dreams.
> You are a scarecrow in a field
> the birds have plundered – useless love.
> Send money; I cannot eat your pink words.

The moon will not believe me.
She says my heart is beating in your vanished hands.

II

This woman walking along the road
keeps seeing her heart fall behind her
bleeding into the buried caul.

This woman walking along the road keeps walking.

Her heart keeps falling away from her.

She roasts the falling heart on tinder fires
to sell to hungry travellers.

She dreams of arms wrapped around arms.

She dreams she is a feather on a flying bird.

She dreams of an enormous mother beckoning her.

She carries her father on her journey's back.

Her stomach is filled with his bones.

She bursts with pain and continues walking.

Her heart drops away, drops away.

She calls 'I love you' in the wind.

The words hang like dead birds around her ears.

She is a stick no one will hold.

      Far away, her name has faded on a man's dry skin.

She lies down on the gravel.

A thorn tree grows through her,
pushing her upright.

III

The woman with the thorn tree growing through her chest arrives in
    the city.
She sees a picture of a house with grass and water,
and a doorway in which people embrace.
She decides to become such a house.
She sits on the sandy floor of the city.

She plucks an orange from the gutter and sells it to a hungry man.

      A man grabs the orange and eats it fast,
      thinking the taste of the woman seller.
      It wasn't enough.

She has six cents in her hand, she shows it to the moon.

IV

The moon curses me, turning away
and I juggle with oranges in the dirt.
I juggle with coins I plaster my skin with hands.
The moon curses me, returning.

Everyone is hungry, every mouth eats me.
I am only so many crumbs of air, a sky
covered with ants, they carry me piece by piece away.
The moon stays, stroking the black bone beneath.

What if I had waited for him on the road?
Moon, you know nothing.
My hands held no offering for him.
I am cursed with myself.

V

Trader in hungers,
she grew strong.

And everything that could be eaten, was eaten.

She was bricks, words, skin, bread.

She was fire, milk, the road, the shade.

Her roof stretched wide across the city.

In her doorway people embraced.

The moon grew thinner and thinner
watching over the wastelands of her abundance.

VI

Ghost against trees, lucent hunger
or thirst? Is it silver water
that would bring you back to me?

I am dry sticks, my love,
and I hunger so for the greenness
of hands on me, I am the carcass of dreams,
you may drift through my spaces.

Where do you sleep,
who do you love,
are you somewhere else a man?
Transparent love, your body
holds my earth and sky,
you are the window open on my drought.

You are a dead ghost.
I am rich and you will eat none of my coins.
You are a memory ghost.
Nothing is promised me.
From hunger to wealth I have come
through the desert of my heart.

The Man with Incomplete Words on his Roof

The man with incomplete words on his roof
haunts the streets in search of additional letters.

Old green letters
and spaces.
His sheet of tin has old green letters and spaces
spread across it.

Someone looking down at the roof
would make no sense of it.

He hunts for more letters that green, that old.
He steals lettered tin
from other people's roofs and walls
trying to find the match.

People wake up with a dog staring at them from the yard
or rain in their hair.
They chase him, they take back their sheets of tin.
Cursing his incomplete roof
they tell him to throw it away, they offer
to buy him a new sheet of tin, plain silver.

No, no.
He wakes each morning from a dream
that the letters have washed away. Sweating, he climbs up
to find them.

His neighbours watch him from their rooms
with missing walls. They talk
of painting over the letters with black paint.

Sometimes they find the sounds of the spaces in their throats.

In the Wind

In the wind her door bangs shut
and then wide open.
Glass crashes.
She isn't here.
She doesn't come home.

Migrant Love

I

He coming home at night
(this is home)
closes his eyes to call her
and sees his grey soul:
a curtain blowing at an open window.

Long ago her arms lay along his arms,
her breath drifted across his breast
like rain, sweet air in the grass.

II

The city at night is a smoky tunnel
yellowed with eyes and voices
she almost recognises.

Where she stands the men come
one by one, almost
his smell.

III

In his streets doorways clutch at him:
he never feels her luminous touch

but the oiled perfumes burning in rooms
encourage his hardening skin to shine.

IV

Deep in the night
she dances desperately upon his lips.
His tongue is wrapped around
a different consolation.
In the morning there is a paleness of dreams on his skin.

Fire and Ash

Good friends huddle over the same fire,
touch night's gloved fingertip to fingertip,
empty their softest laughter out for kindling,
carve gifts out of the stories of their lives,

trace shadows in the ground of fearful thoughts,
offer each other almost all their crying,
lean a forehead on a winter shoulder,
lock arms and sleep in the red glow.

But in the knife-edge morning each is curled
around a distance, like a winter bird
ash-grey and frozen
inside its silence: waking
they stare at the hard space between them,
pull their coats tight, turn away.

Needle Work

From my needle small birds fly:
pink lattice feathers, leafgreen eyes,
yellow crests, plum spikes for tails.

Beside me on the metal pole
tubing threads down from a plastic bag
as thick and soft as a pound of liver:

your blood, midnight red stitches
of the deep needle filling you;
mine chainstitching bright birds.

Black Eagles

They circle the hot mountain
and when the time comes
she rises in a slow spiral
calling him with her wingbeat,
her deep wingbeat breath,
her wingbeat rising in the blue air
higher and higher.

He waits for her, calling her
up to the crest of the long descent:
she turns on her back and falls,
wings wide under his lowering shadow
coming down onto her,
into her falling flight.

Wing upon wing they fuse with the light
flaring around their beating hearts,
falling, falling into the fire
lifting their tongues for the cry of arrival.

Poem for Someone who Died
(M.H. – 21/5/89)

who died?
she died
anybody could have died
but she died

many roses were dispersed
across the sand
where she died
anybody could have died

in a hole
beneath the oyster-catchers' feet
a yellow bag of ash is buried
who died?
no one, no one

who called her back?
no one

the petals scooped the ashes up
and sailed out on the tide
after she died

He is Looking for Her

When everyone had gone, he came back to the place,
got down on his knees in the sand, and dug
to fetch her out.

He dug deeper than any burying spade had gone,
up to his armpits in live sand
but only the small white crabs ran out through his fingers.

He moved on, digging with his hands
the whole length of the lagoon, weeping for her,
tearing up the earth.

She touches his ear with her breath, calling:
Look up, look up, I am flying on the updraught
of the emerald-breasted honeycatcher's wingbeat,
look up, my darling, I escaped at once.

He heard nothing, digging through his heart:
she is waiting for him to look up.

At Midnight Everything

everything is important and the seagulls
use the streetlamps as fishing nets
for their delicate moth dinners
and paving stones are deathly cold
for glue-drunk children at midnight, cars glare
along the hungry roads and the mist sinks
into polystyrene egg boxes tumbled in alleys
across the sleeping city and everything is important
and those who have left will never return

Countries

Ancestors

Clues

1. Outside it snows
    and horsemen ride in with guns.
    An old man in a prayer shawl
    sips tea through a sugar cube.

    If he had looked up
    he would have seen through the doorway
    a small child standing in sunlight far away
    waving to him: he might have waved back.

2. Women laughing in a hot kitchen
    unto the last generation.

3. On a train someone sits, weeping,
    eating the last bread from her mother's hand.

4. They looked back from the deck of a ship
    at the quay. Strangers watched them go.

    They remember only their own voices.
    Here are no graves to visit.

5. Two lit candles.
    Gold words embroidered on blue velvet.
    Sweet wine.

6. Grodno, 1850.
    Khar'kov, 1990.

7. Shepherd over bare rock,
    Cloth merchants.
    Owners of books.
    Men who wore waistcoats.
    Women who died young.

8. The wheatear and the tern go back.
    They return without messages.

9.   The child holds a cobweb of old wedding lace
     and a small string of grey pearls.

     She places her ear against sepia lips, waiting.

The Water Carrier

I
in the amniotic waters she swam and swam
expanding her ocean

outside they heard the heartbeat
of their little promise: they held out their cold hands, ready:

outside she shrivelled to a silent shell,
polite, hid from grown-ups, didn't answer questions

they cloaked her and cloaked her, she walked
carefully, child monarch under the cutting crown,
brace on the curved spine

II
they saw a shadow swim into the lamplit room
in the passage everything was night quiet

they stood over her bed, watching:
she curled like a mask around her heart

III
in the dark she opened
inside her weightless veils of magic,
swam out to where they couldn't see her:
loved them with her whole self. wept because they couldn't see her

IV
she woke in the curtained room:
outside there was already a day in their hands,
laughing heat of their tongues

she sobbed: ice child in her abandoned ocean, dead

Baptism

wild green sand blue wind cloaks the dunes and dugout caves
beyond the ragged gravel road scattered with old clothes

in this vagrant landscape people sleep briefly,
pass through or disintegrate here

> But in the centre is her house,
> a small brick square squatting
> sturdy as a pig or a tank.
> Inside are small square rooms
> filled with her achievements:
> the lounge suite, the wall unit, the music centre,
> many moulded plastic pictures of happiness,
> cards that say A Mother is the Heart of the House
> and You Are My Love, a three-part wooden object
> displaying three parts of a Christian message
> hung down the wall on a red ribbon,
> two dolls dressed in hundreds of blue feathers
> like queens or carnival dancers.
>
> In the middle of the room her little daughter
> is fixed in a red metal ring that walks if she moves.
> All the grown-ups look down at her, smiling.
> The wind is blowing loudly outside.
> Bits of sand hit the window panes.

Night Travellers

In the back seat I squeezed against the door
as two strangers joined us in the dark.
The woman spread her shawl over me.
She wore a smokey moon on a chain.

'Go to sleep,' my mother said.
The man's hand stroked my hair.
When I woke up it was nearly light
and the air around me was still warm.

I looked back to where they were walking
into the veld, taller than trees.
Tears were rising in my chest.
'Go to sleep,' my mother said. 'We're not there yet.'

Countries

the first one is nature
it waits for you it places you between stars
it names you it buries itself in your endocrine gardens

the next and the next and the next
are choices yours or someone else's
and you see your loose edges forever
hanging over oceans, letting the cold air blow in
to drum the membrane of the first original only
home
echo of your natural self

Hope for Refugees

you can go back
you can go back
run backwards
call back the cattle
unstitch the hems
pull the photos out of the fire

you can go back
you can go back
pull down your dress
button your shirt
wipe off the blood
scrub off the blood

you can go back
you can go back
wash the walls
fix the door
remember the step down in the dark
avoid the dark

you can go back
you can go back
dig up the box in the front garden
dig up the box in the yard
dig up the box in your heart
dig up the box in the child's heart

you can go back
you can go back
lay out the skeletons in their beds
hang out the years to air
plant seeds, keep watch at the well
tear up your nightmares, your footprints
lock the door
work hard
give thanks to god

She Takes One Suitcase with Her

on my shoulder air weighs
more than the sun on the trees
and my hair lifts up to display
jewels from a cave, green jewels from a cave

night is the memory of day
I am the memory of light
blue is the sky on my forehead
amber the words of my flight

Application for Naturalization

Country.
Could your mountainous days ever fold around my arrival?
I wait in a room with blank walls that wait.
I go out among the sea, the streets, the sky:
they are too busy to make conversation.

Country:
must I become dust for your moonlight to drink?
You don't open my window.
I lean against the glass,
I hear you talking to the gulls all night.

I am luminous, not transparent,
a spell waiting to be uttered.
Country, become my shadow,
I will become your body.

Pangaea

Home,
it's called:
where you can find your way in the dark.

Somewhere else it could be
what you remember,
your ashes in the hearth.

Once all the continents were joined –
can you imagine?
Everyone walked in the same forest.

*'Home was the centre of the world because it was the place where a
vertical line crossed with a horizontal one. The vertical line was a path
leading upwards to the sky and downwards to the underworld. The
horizontal line represented the traffic of the world, all the possible
roads . . . Thus, at home, one was nearest to the gods in the sky and to
the dead in the underworld. This nearness promised access to both.
And at the same time, one was at the starting point and, hopefully, the
returning point of all terrestrial journeys.'* – John Berger

The emigrants carried on their backs
the cross of their necessities.
But worn with long journeying
the vertical and horizontal swayed like booms in a headwind.
Graves, doors, voices, gods slipped off along the way,
crumbs falling on the route out
swallowed by exile's firm valve.
When they arrived their pasts were completely empty.

In time their industry produced new vertical
ladders between a bed and a suitcase
and their horizontals became
the mass of them stretching back and forward,
their road through the world the sum of their own
displacement, so wide and long
all the continents are joined again.

Home,
it's called.

I who Live Here, It is I

'This earth was the first to speak.
I have been pronounced once and for all.'
    – Breyten Breytenbach, *Return to Paradise*

I
In my sleep I return here.

*

Being here, giving birth to my city I am
day by day being home, day by day
it has no name, seeds came from all parts of the known world
to plant me here, being myself these rooms, streets, rain, tides,
the air tasting of me, cool mist my hair, my skin hot stone,
the pulsing of hands my hands growing sand and wood
as the sky enters my eyes and the sea wells from my feet
and I turning inside out disappear into all manner of joyous bird cries
and the weeping of engines and wind,
gulls and avid rats feed where I feed,
consuming this limitless home swelling inside me
as I inside it open wide enough to die.

*

Coming home I see it coming towards me,
rubbing against me like a welcoming cat.

In my sleep I feel it leaning against me, sleeping.

*

Dried apricots, soft and sour
dawn wind stings the palm tree.

35

Neon rivers spilling across
the smell of buses pushing homeward.

*

In my sleep I return here.

II

It is only one look, one acrid glance shearing across the sweet blue hour
and the air pulls back, embarrassed at its intimacy,
leaving me naked as a captured slave, a trespasser, a thief.

All people ask: what are you doing here? what are you?
Eyes and eyes and eyes, scraping my shadow off all surfaces.

Any person here rebukes me.
Any person here in the streets of my home rebukes me.
I, walking like a strange person in the streets of my home
stare at my footsteps spread out on the road and deny them.
Any person is more at home here than I am.

The walls and the wind withdraw obediently from my skin.
I breathe in the bitter juice of any person looking at me,
peeling me off the air, expelling me.

All people live in my home and say it is not me, it is not,
all people invite me in and say look, it is not yours, welcome.

Any person has permission because of history.
Because of justice. Because of songs of genesis.
Any person being decidedly here in my self
banishes me. Any person refuses permission.
Any person who says nothing, or everything.
does not say my name. Any person is here in my place,
it is not my place.
How is it that my born home
is loyal to anyone who passes
in the street, following him like a hot beast
eager for better origins?

III

They say if my name were found here
buried in rock older and older
than any home a person can recall,
my home would return to me.

But no name is my home.
I am spread wider over the sand
than the width of a name.
Being born here the cells of my skin
are all the time of history.

What voice could pronounce the whole tide of my days?
What eyes could pour sky into my sky?

If this could be, if anyone here
were here with me inside the water and the wind
my home would flow through me and through anyone
and return to me, return to me in my sleep.

Humus

Without words or plans I was arriving
led by the surf, the days, the small streets and balconies,
worms and beetles came to fetch me,
by the waters of my homeless years I lay down gratefully,
ocean salts drifted in over my lips,
my eyelashes left like yachts on a further journey

I lay down, settling
so deep down, crumbling like bread
or the source of roses, honey, eggs

One by one my cells set out through tiny mouths,
atoms I knew moved along twigs, perched
on the tip of a thorn over some bird's wing feathers,
close enough to smell its arrival

Curiously my genes made proposals:
now the dune grass sings in a familiar voice,
a bed of succulents has grown pale and thoughtful,
the parapet of a building flicks its hair in the sun

All the while I lie here inside the seasons
watching the endless generosity of my bones,
mornings and planets keep coming to fetch me

Return

Voluntary Removal

While the truck churns the dirt impatiently
under its load of destitute furniture,
while men with papers stamp their feet,
while children howl and dogs run away to the hills,
the old man stares and stares through a window frame
in the last wall standing
at a blue dazzle of sea rising to greet him.

'Come old man, come old man!'
The men call, the sea calls.
'Come old man!'

He comes from the house lifting his empty hands
to his face, he takes his old hands
and removes his eyes, he comes forward to the sea
to leave his eyes there,
and the truck may remove his body.

Dispossessed Words

found poem

for Jessie Tamboer, who set herself alight and burned to death
because she could no longer provide food for her children

Trucks carried 40,000 blacks to the southern edge of the desert.
I cannot say anything about my future now.
      We had a very beautiful view
      and this was the first time I saw my father cry.

They said 'Old man, are you moving?'
I took a crowbar, pulled the house down.
I cannot say anything about my future now.

    *

    A man must have a dumping ground.
    Every rabbit has got a warren.
    A native must have a warren too.

    *

Sometimes I cry, I
the absolute poor
I am sick to death of watching my ruin.

    *

We had a very beautiful view of the sea –
      This was refused.

    *

Uncovering the rubbish bins, I ask, could it not be
that something has been thrown in here –
just a little something that I can chew?

This was refused.

    *

42

At times she would just suddenly start sobbing without any apparent
   reason.

The absence of love.
There is no way you can describe that hunger.
Shining clean pots and jars:
There was no food whatsoever in the house.

                 *

She was immediately engulfed by flames but did not utter a sound
as she walked around the yard burning.

The ashes of one household are collected by another for the bits of coal.
If you want to survive you must make a plan.

I cannot say anything about my future now.

Days

'In poverty boredom hangs like a dark cloud. Despair.'

If there is a tree I sit under it.
Or a piece of tin roof. Shade instead of water.
He rides the blue train.* I drink the dust.
Clouds and clouds, the day going somewhere,
shapes to think about.
My head won't lift up. Pebbles, pebbles. Ground.

Morning.
Afternoon.

The sun is on the wall, then on the mountain.
The ground is cold, then hot.

It is evening.
He is gone on the blue train.
I get up, I go into the house, lie down on the floor.
He left the last coach of the train for me.
If I drink it I hope I will go away.

---

* Methylated spirits

Freedom's Hostage

on the release of Nelson Mandela into South Africa ·

corner of the century poured out onto sand
icon of power buried in a well
slow turtle hatching ancient eggs
phoenix wrapped in tongues
cargo-ship on the dusk horizon
name branded on the air
delicate memory of hope
gas seeping into the valley
magician in a blind cell

       outside your house there is a mountain
       of petitions from ten million souls

       beyond the gate they are building a crucifix

       tall comrade in a tailored suit
       freedom requires that you step forward

Leader

In these plague nights he lays his body open
to the infinite small creatures needing his blood.

The air is dense with mists of sentiment
circling the mounds of opalescent eggs
laid upon altars, over graves, along the great road,
lifting their silvery mucous like wedding veils.

Inside each one, foetal and perfectly formed,
power grows with the softness of insect wings,
incubating in the sweet clouds that thicken
over his open body.

Reclaiming our Land

Every map is out of date.
The roads go to unbuilt houses.
How do the tortoises know
there's bush on the far side of the tar?

At night stars fall like gooseberries,
one into my lap, one into your lap,
husked in cosmic permissions.
Everyone gets a star.
Soon there'll be none left.
You have to eat it; they aren't for planting.

Put up a mirror where you are
and make yourself at home in your familiar eyes.
Outside the wind blew it all away.

Return

Think of the long green road unfolding,
the shadowy wind in the bush along the way,
the sun dancing backwards before you
towards the horizon's powdery veil.

Think of those waiting, the fearsome beloved,
their dreams laid out for you to kiss.
They have written the dance
you must dance on your arrival.

Think of the wide relentless air
open around your arrowed return,
and of your certain, foreign silhouette
diffusing to dust in this vast desert, home.

Riders in the Storm

The walls breathe in the wind
deeply and its energy swirls inside me,
the tan tien region of the room.
Now black voices advertise school socks
on the white kids' music channel. Shifts, shifts.
Blue light like a flashbulb flares on the piano's black skin.
The clouds are heavy grey hunting grandfathers out there
in the night sky. Things are breaking and blowing away.
Gusts come closer, louder.
The windows push themselves tighter shut.
The bottom of the curtain flaps and frills like a dancing dress
in a graveyard. Turning the music up very loud helps.
A white voice cuts the blues with a request to make peace happen.
The building is shaking.
The palm tree's leaves flail above its stumpy unresponding trunk.
The howls are fierce inside me.
Come back Jim Morrison, louder.

A Small Nervous Woman

A small nervous woman walks between a dark man
bedding down on flattened cartons behind a low barrier
of empty fruitboxes in a doorway smiling at her, and a dark
man in a dinner suit under the golden pillars of an evening
hotel, putting his hands in his pockets as she passes,
and thinks
who are my friends?
why is the world so explicit?
what can my heart change?

49

Africa was Good to Them

Rabbi Vermilion was praying privately
in the empty synagogue when Joe Ndzimbi knocked
on the door and walked in saying, 'I need sanctuary.
You must hide me.' 'I'm praying, can't you wait?'
said Rabbi Vermilion. 'No,' said Joe,
'carry on praying' and walked into the Ark
drawing the curtain behind him. He thrust out his hand,
waving something at Rabbi Vermilion and said,
'Here this is good luck for you' and withdrew.
It was a small box beetle, glittering green with black eyes
and a carapace like a Fabergé emerald egg.
It sat on the Rabbi's pulpit and said, 'We can go
to Jerusalem or Atlantis, where would you prefer?'
and Rabbi Vermilion to his eternal credit and damnation
said Atlantis. Now he moves like a dolphin through
the old streets deep down, so happy he knows he is
someone else. Joe is still hiding in the Ark, thinking
angrily that the box beetle never offered him any choices.

City Sundowner

spread out
come in
catch a tiger by its gleam
vortex neatly
into the carpool
it's sundowner time
pink, purple and orange
with a cherry, spread out
sit still or the stars will bite
sit still
sit still
you're spreading
where does this skin stop?
come in put on your jacket
do come in
do
why is the sky flesh-coloured?
pour me a sundowner
that tiger's splashing the horizon
the air feels like fire on my arms
where are my arms?
what does that tiger have in its mouth?
spread out
soft cherry

Enough

She has her straight communion with God
on a long cord that shortens twice a year,
but normally her world is round and more upholstered than the desert.
She has no thoughts for the expanding dark
outside the window because she suffers from vertigo
but lying awake thinking of the caretaker's death is pain enough
and how many millions of people can one person grieve for
day in and day out, worried that her books won't balance?
She has to lock the door at night, she's alone.

Welcome

soldiers and stockbrokers
shake hands:
there are no sides any more

bananas are growing on the pear tree
a satisfied cat flicks its tail
in the cream
        three black hairs float there

volcanic sunsets bleed over toasting lovers
the ice-cream man collects unused condoms
the cars drive straight upward
on the mountain sliding into the sea
the speaking totem pole in the sky
is called Nelson

bananas are growing on the pear tree
a yellow bag full of pink notes
sails down the cableway
little hands open and close like venus flytraps
black ones

there's snow everywhere
the roads are melting
welcome home, exiles and entertainers
you get three shares in a pear tree
a bullet and a banana
to help you settle in: shake hands

Summertime

The new South Africa's two years old
and more's been lost than we've been told.
No jobs, no rain, no foreign aid,
no hopes, no dreams, no victory parade.
But one commodity's still around:
the summertime white boys turning brown.

In blaring cars with surfboard racks,
with designer T-shirts on their backs,
they come as they've done for twenty years
untouched by doubts or political fears.
They're perennial holiday season flowers,
these summertime white boys turning brown.

Despite the drought and the ozone hole
they find enough beer and suntan oil
to keep them bearing B. Comm. fruit
and growing to fit the manager's suit
in every business in every town,
the summertime white boys turning brown.

There's still enough time for them to buy
the meat they need for the last beach braai,
and the unit trusts and Kruger rands
and investment stakes in distant lands
that they'll take with them on the autumn flight
as the nation fills up with brown boys turning white.

Can't Stand, Can't Dance

No one's nailed down properly here.
There's always a corner loose and we wobble
bending over to hold it down.
There are these things down there –
id, morals, a national heart, keys –
sifting and circling as insistent gusts
lift that corner all the time. Other things blow in
and we have to keep checking
what's going on underneath
but we can't go all the way down
because
the other foot's hammered down fiercely over stones
that we own with grimacing pride,
determined proprietors of our birthright.
We're these cramped goblins hobbled to our accumulated selves,
holding up fistfuls of soil for balance:
can't stand, can't dance,
can't take a chance on an arabesque
in the space rolling past our borders.

Statues

Some lonely men stand around this city
petrified in difficult moments.

They have the eyes of people who never felt love,
so alone, achieving the country.

The people they achieved never notice them,
the contradictory pulling of muscles inside the metal.

Like stray outcroppings of rock.
It's impossible to believe they were ever the cause of anything.

This, Too

The child's fingers breaking the wings at the joint
thrill with the feathery heat of the bird's pain.

Pushing the axe through bone, amazed
a man sees his hands glow with the life running into them.

This woman cuts her flesh with steel and lies back
watching her mysterious red agony escape.

Who placed shackles on the human repertoire?
Killing gives pleasure, dying is half our skill.
This we can do, with voice and heart and will.

I Holding Open my Hand

I holding open my hand
where the memory is sprouting
could be offering
(look how the black roots spread like telephone wires)
or perhaps simply demonstrating
(my legs rise and I float sideways beside my hand)
what little control I have
eyes have made homes in this memory
chattering like starlings all over my palm
I thought this might happen and it's happening
in the drought the roots are fattening
and these birds are all staring at me
as if I could teach them to drink

Presence

flung asteroid crumbling
I condense this cavernous moment
to gold mist settling,
          overflowing

magnet eye holding the universe
still, now such tender atoms
open their wet wings
dissolving their glistening unpeeled light
in memory

          as the blue fish resting
at the zenith of its leap, the blade halfway
through the cow's neck, the bullet basking
in its sunlit trajectory, the buckle
unclasping

Incarnate Eternity

arrive screaming
in this blood-birth
steel and the roses in my eyes
nor any grief will still me
not for your most holy suffering will I lay down
my wings in this necessary massacre
with all my life seizing the jasmine growing
from the hole where they raped me
how it grows and grows

                    *

                                        (that pastel hope
                                        is an old sweet wrapper:
                                        burn it, your teeth are stained
                                        with mourning)

                    *

blood is good for you
it is above all something red and liquid
like a strawberry in a shaft of sunlight

it wells up through bones and tissue
clotted with boundaries of hair and white fluids
this is the place the sun hides at night
bring it out, melt my hands with it

the ritual is to pour a cup
of someone's blood onto the land,
this is your way of claiming your home,
your political truth, your existence

kiss me, my lips are full of it,
I live here

                    *

red river, you smell of freedom
as the new grass smells of my father's bones

                    *

my arm uncurls
and I am holding for you
grown out of all the spores of my generations
the green territory of the fern they planted in my kloof –
look how the red drops from it!

                    *

it is
the bridge of blood   two little souls crossing under a parasol
the barrier of blood   the tidal wave is a wall of fish
the big red full stop   the maize grows so tall this yellow year
the juice of vote papers   beetles scavenge like jewels
quickred
seasalted
here even the shadows bleed
especially the shadows bleed
dark sponges of history
birds suck from them
in the drought growing fat, red

                    *

To be here is my breast in my hand
aimed at you, my cannibal happiness,
your wail dismembering the road
but when the red train passes into my tunnel
something opens : time : silence
the linear serenity of air against this cool mountain
space beyond blood, my ocean spreads.

Abandon me to this blue present.

Where I sit permanence shimmers
and my heart is a cave the birds leave and enter.
Now you may slice off my head,
my neck spills pearls and the breath of whales,
my spine rolls against a silver hand,
my fingers are grains of sand.
This beak pecking my lips
this beak pecking my lips
draws blood whose blood is in me
how did the ocean get this red?

                    *

We are showing ourselves to ourselves
the people of our future
agonies of half-bodies
watching each other across a blade.
Are you lost? come home now.

The human hand can exert force of eight litres per bullet
and so light on its toes.

Oh mother, mother, why are you crying?
She looks just like you.
Here, let me take this blood off your lap.

                    *

        Sit absolutely still
        as they sever your selves
        sit absolutely still
        bleed precisely downwards
        concentrate your spirit
        into this pillar of memory
        no one passing through
        will survive.

I have been walking   I have been sitting on one side
I have been watching   I have been waiting on one side
I have been undoing   I have been in the water
I have been not waiting   I have been walking
I have been unfolding   I have been filling my shadow

here it comes
I had no name for calling it
here it comes
red juice of the future
pouring me out

what can you do?
can you do this, too?
faster, faster

*

Homework:

categories:

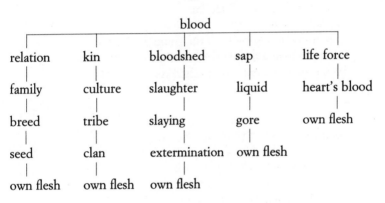

blood

relation	kin	bloodshed	sap	life force
family	culture	slaughter	liquid	heart's blood
breed	tribe	slaying	gore	own flesh
seed	clan	extermination	own flesh	
own flesh	own flesh	own flesh		

Tiresias in the City of Heroes

I IN THE CITY OF HEROES

Not only the unexploded bombs in their hearts
but these sweet pools of honey in each pair of hands
cupped to sip, being
a past that lit the night all the way to this
ending: dry air in a still, old city.

Memories are the daylight, in a place with no present.
The map with the closed rooms along the way unfolded
and you arrived with all the closed rooms in your years
throbbing, you arrived beyond the boundary of your map
saying, here I am, and from the closed rooms
such voices answered you: here I am.

If they had known the script
these heroes in the city of heroes
would have become statues and stopped waiting.

As it is they sat so still all day
but not – composed,
something in the angles of the amputated limbs
always implying movement of the ghost of movement,
even though absent, not finished yet

                    *

waiting.

                    *

Over the square the pale dust of the dry season sifts;
from jacarandas and flamboyants desiccated petals
in the victory colours fall.
Air murmurs.

The jungle licks the walls on the home side;
reticent waves attend at the outer edge.

The ground transmits biographies
of movement and hesitation,
vibrations of uneven footsteps circling
this city, this transit camp, this photograph of the time
before the end of struggle,
souvenir of the old days,
still breathing.

The jungle rustles with satisfied laughter.
It opens no path, yields no messenger,
darker and darker green, ancient.

      *

After the war there are always heroes
to be forgotten until they are dead.
There can be no heroes in times of peace.
Inside every song the words are buried:
Stay away, heroes of our struggles.
Let us paint pictures of you, let us tell stories.
Stay away where we can imagine you.
If you return now you will crumble like ancient kings
untombed in our corrosive air.

      *

These are not refugees, good god –
it isn't help they need, coins and crutches.
These men and women left in a column of fire
and will return garlanded with their deeds.
These men and women went in order to return,
not fleeing they were singing the jungles open,
setting up mirrors all the way to look back,
to send light and their faces back to the homeland
waiting for their deeds to arrive.
Not seeing the jungle grow up in their mirrors
new and permanent.

      *

What do I remember? Standing in the sun for hours listening to speeches while my feet burned on the ground. Walking along streets where women stood at every door crying. Hacked bodies. A little man who followed me for three kilometres and when I finally tried to grab him he begged me to teach him to sing, but I thought he was lying and killed him. A baby with its stomach carved out and a policeman standing next to it, vomiting. Being given a computer and told to write. The smell of beer on dead men's lips. Sitting in a shebeen drinking brandy after brandy and getting so happy I felt like flying. A woman laughing as another woman's house burned down. Yellow cars and vans: that thick flat yellow like sweet icing on a cake. The noise of helicopters. My mother saying don't go, or don't come back. My child screaming when I tried to pick him up. Meat roasting at my child's funeral. A book with my photo in it. Crowds becoming silent. A man who shot his wife in a meeting. The noise of helicopters. My burning feet. Bodies in the street covered in blankets. My home is place I'm frightened of. It's a big sore inside me that burns when I touch it.

'Are you not bigger than your own backyard?
In that war each of us became the nation:
the whole nation entered into each of us.
Tell us that story.'

That story. That story:
In Sharpeville your arms died.
In Uitenhage your tongues died.
In Boipatong your eyes died.
In Katlehong and Bekkersdal and Empangeni
you died and you died and you died.
That's what I remember.

In Pretoria your fingernails became joint chief of staff.
In Pretoria your teeth ran the central bank.
In Pretoria your hair was the president.
That's what I remember.

In Jo'burg you heart was tortured and died.
In Cape Town your skin joined the enemy police.
In the veld and the mountains your memory buried its children.
That's what I remember.

These heroes are heroes,
triumphant on the long, long way home,
their silent days in this city
are a journey and it will end.

>   And they will become kings and queens in their own land,
>   and multitudes will welcome them
>   with candles and flowers and firstborn children
>   to bless with their golden pain.

>   *

II TIRESIAS REMEMBERS

A man came, unfortunate bridge. Tiresias:
with his dangerous memory come to the city of heroes.
Foolish man, looking for a woman
to watch her say again, go away.
Melting memories into dreams with a blind longing,
the hot longing that opens darkness,
melting the dreams of heroes into memories,
aching, aching.

>   *

A man arriving is an emissary or an enemy.
Tiresias holds his poor broken heart under the shedding jacaranda
as the heroes undo him with questions.

'Tell us the story of the war we won.'
Like children looking for a history to wear.

That's what I remember.
All this dead and defeated is your story.
Only the hair and the shadow still growing,
responding to sunlight, and I ask myself
which body were they grafted onto in that moment of darkness
before total victory was declared?
My home is a place I'm frightened of.

The heroes leave him in the marketplace
like an old newspaper, blurred with the truth,
sifting the dry breeze for her scent.

*

In a cool room she lies on the mourning mat.
Themba, he says, Themba, Themba.
You are still here.

You are still here, she says with the voice of dead bullets.
He is gone and you are still here.
Why couldn't they kill you?

*

There's nothing to remember.
What remains is here.
Its origins will repeat themselves.
How this man got his power
and that man starves
will not glue joy to your heart.
Sing or dream
or keep silent inside your bandages.
Don't dig, it only cuts the roots
and whatever is growing now will wither
like what came before.
Silence is big enough to hold the present
wide open for you to breathe in.

*

III TO SAVE WHAT MUST BE SAVED

Heroes are those who will kill to save what must be saved.

Mnyaniso comes to the doorstep where Tiresias sits
carrying the knife, the long curved blade, a hook for a man's heart.
Once before he has excised a heart from his body
unmarked and fresh, a bulb stored in the dark room
of his return.

'Ah, Mnyaniso, do you remember
how as a child you could carve open the stem of a lily
without snapping it? How the lily continued to grow,
receiving its sap in two rivers now instead of one?'

'We could do such things, such things, Tiresias,
such expansions of the spirit in us.
Now my hand is a vulture on my dead days.'

'But remember, Mnyaniso, remember your hand, remember.'

All night Mnyaniso cut the bougainvillea petals,
and in the morning Tiresias was a tree
with a million blood-red birds singing in its branches.

Chaos Theory

THE DIALECTICS OF LOVE AND UNCLES

All the way down there are conditions
to fall over the edge of, expeditions
of cells ferning in turns curving on
down over the edge and falling on
over the farther edge.

A serious bird pecks at the scruff of a winter palm
the day after its feathery intentions have unfolded, calmly
triangulating Darwin and Marx two billion years along God's graph.
Between mouthfuls, a claw intercepts some dust
from a transitory planet's path
and whirls its way into a dragon's seed.
Nothing will ever be the same again in that family.

Necessary if not sufficient, this bifurcating hour
digs a road through history and a tower,
frothing in diamond drops over the edge of order.
Like a tiara unravelling, said the queen's warder.

And oh, my love, this crystal fire makes you more warm
than anything my breast has known these many centuries.
Stay with me as my words fly through the waterfall.
A breath to left or right could wake the dragon's need
uncurling in a fresh grain of time.

Now here its uncle is again, this memory of a dinosaur,
fat-voiced on a cold day, triumphant over the cousin on the sour-berried
    tree.
Stuck on the dispossessed tendril of the graph, all he can hope for
is a fractal kiss turning him like a key.

Still you continue unfurling your strange attractors,
the ones the ants around the sugar bowl obey,
curving up the edge of upwards –
and I the sugar in the ants' tears,
tumbling out along my own spiralling love
up over the upwards of your unmapped laughter.

PURPOSEFULLY PEELING FOOTSTEPS

Words are such thin shavings of the fractal fruit,
tiny scrapings of the skin that holds
these joyously determined swirls of history
inside their juicy turbulence.

Talking itself westward after the day's feast,
each little word with its meaning strapped to its back
falls down the swell of tomorrow
like a hiker with hopeful new shoes.

THE FOSSIL'S AUTOBIOGRAPHY (ABRIDGED)

History's tank was mowing
down my resistance.
I was about to be

gone for good.
A smudge
embedded in a stone.

The stone that twitches
under each new plough
sowing freedom for strangers.

Anyone who'd walked
along the vector of my defeat
would have seen

me, leaping up, alive
going under and hopeful, insistently
eating the sunlight in the rising wheat.

All particles of my eradication
continue
flaring inside the hardening rock,
striking sparks off the future's dull blade,
not
quite
gone
yet.
Watch your step.